Lions

By Mary Molly Shea

Gareth Stevens
Publishing

Please visit our Web site, www.garethstevens.com. For a free color catalog of all our high-quality books, call toll free 1-800-542-2595 or fax 1-877-542-2596.

Library of Congress Cataloging-in-Publication Data

Shea, Mary Molly.
  Lions / Mary Molly Shea.
      p. cm. – (Animals that live in the grasslands)
  Includes index.
  ISBN 978-1-4339-3873-3 (pbk.)
  ISBN 978-1-4339-3874-0 (6-pack)
  ISBN 978-1-4339-3872-6 (library binding)
  1. Lion–Juvenile literature. I. Title.
  QL737.C23S5316 2011
  599.757–dc22

                                                    2010008461

First Edition

Published in 2011 by
Gareth Stevens Publishing
111 East 14th Street, Suite 349
New York, NY 10003

Copyright © 2011 Gareth Stevens Publishing

Designer: Michael J. Flynn
Editor: Therese Shea

Photo credits: Cover, pp. 1, 5, 7, 9, 11, 13, 15, 17, 19, 21, back cover Shutterstock.com.

Printed in the United States of America

CPSIA compliance information: Batch #CS10GS: For further information contact Gareth Stevens, New York, New York at 1-800-542-2595.

Table of Contents

Boldface words appear in the glossary.

King of the Grasslands

Do you know what animal is the "king of beasts"? The lion is! Lions are powerful hunters in the African **grasslands**.

A lion's coat may be yellow, gray, or brown. A **male** lion's big, thick mane makes it look royal. **Female** lions don't have manes.

female

male

mane

A Lion's Pride

Most big cats live alone. However, lions live in groups called prides. A pride is made up of many females, their cubs, and a few males.

pride

Male lions guard the pride's land. They mark the **territory** with their smell. They chase other lions away. They don't want others taking their food.

Female lions are often the hunters of the pride. They hunt **antelopes**, zebras, **wildebeests**, and other large animals. Lions mostly hunt at night.

A lion roars as it begins its hunt. Other members of the pride hear and join the hunt. Often several lions work together to catch an animal.

A mother lion usually has two to four cubs at one time. Lion cubs have dark spots on their coat to help them hide in the grass. They lose their spots as they get older.

cub

Growing Up

Lion cubs begin to hunt when they are about 11 months old. Female lions stay with the pride their whole life.

Male lions stay with the pride 2 to 4 years. Sometimes other males make them leave. They may have to fight to join another pride.

Fast Facts

Height	up to 4 feet (1.2 meters)
Length	up to 6.5 feet (2 meters); tail is up to 40 inches (1 meter)
Weight	up to 500 pounds (225 kilograms)
Diet	antelopes, zebras, wildebeests, and other large animals
Average life span	up to 10 years in the wild

Glossary

antelope: a four-legged animal with hoofs and horns that lives in Africa and Asia

female: a girl

grasslands: land on which grass is the main kind of plant life

male: a boy

territory: an area of land

wildebeest: an animal with a mane, beard, horns, and tail that lives in Africa

For More Information

Books

Bodden, Valerie. *Lions*. Mankato, MN: Creative Education, 2010.

Joubert, Beverly, and Dereck Joubert. *Face to Face with Lions*. Washington, DC: National Geographic, 2008.

Web Sites

Lion

www.awf.org/content/wildlife/detail/lion
Read more about lion prides and the greatest danger to lions—people.

Lions

kids.nationalgeographic.com/Animals/ CreatureFeature/Lion
Print out a picture of a lion, and see a video of a lion in action.

Index

About the Author

Mary Molly Shea, a practicing nurse and forensic scientist, spends her free time rescuing animals in western New York and doing research for books like this one.